HOW ROBERTA VINCI
STUNNED SERENA

UNDERDOGS

CHAMPIONS

★
★
★

BY MARTIN G

45TH PARALLEL PRESS

Published in the United States of America by Cherry Lake Publishing Group
Ann Arbor, Michigan
www.cherrylakepublishing.com

Reading Adviser: Beth Walker Gambro, MS, Ed., Reading Consultant, Yorkville, IL
Series Adviser: Virginia Loh-Hagan
Book Designer: Jen Wahi

Photo Credits: cover: © Leonard Zhukovsky/Shutterstock; page 5: © Diliff, CC BY 3.0 via Wikimedia Commons; page 7: © Leonard Zhukovsky/Shutterstock; page 9: © Phil Anthony/Shutterstock; page 13: © Leonard Zhukovsky/Shutterstock; page 15: © robbiesaurus from Smithtown, NY, USA, CC BY-SA 2.0, via Wikimedia Commons; page 19: © Tourism Victoria, CC BY 2.0, via Wikimedia Commons; page 23: © Leonard Zhukovsky/Shutterstock; page 27: © Leonard Zhukovsky/Shutterstock; page 29: © Paul Cowan/Shutterstock

45th Parallel Press is an imprint of Cherry Lake Publishing Group.

Library of Congress Cataloging-in-Publication Data

Names: Gitlin, Marty, author.
Title: How Roberta Vinci stunned Serena / written by Martin Gitlin.
Description: Ann Arbor, Michigan : 45th Parallel Press, 2023. | Series:
  Underdogs. Sports champions | Audience: Grades 4-6 | Summary: "How
  Roberta Vinci Stunned Serena takes readers inside the famous U.S. Open
  match between Roberta Vinci and Serena Williams. Provides background
  leading up to the match, review of the match, why the world was shocked,
  and what happened afterward. From players no one believed in to teams no
  one thought could win, Underdogs: Sports Champions covers some of
  history's greatest underdogs. Written in a strong narrative nonfiction
  style, the storytelling in these books will captivate readers. The
  series includes considerate vocabulary, engaging content, clear text and
  formatting, and compelling photos. Educational sidebars include extra
  fun facts and information"-- Provided by publisher.
Identifiers: LCCN 2023005871 | ISBN 9781668927748 (hardcover) | ISBN
  9781668928790 (paperback) | ISBN 9781668930267 (ebook) | ISBN
  9781668931745 (pdf)
Subjects: LCSH: Vinci, Roberta, 1983---Juvenile literature. | Williams,
  Serena, 1981---Juvenile literature. | U.S. Open (Tennis
  tournament)--Juvenile literature.
Classification: LCC GV994.V55 G57 2023 | DDC 796.342092/52
  [B]--dc23/eng/20230306
LC record available at https://lccn.loc.gov/2023005871

Cherry Lake Publishing would like to acknowledge the work of the Partnership for 21st Century Learning, a network of Battelle for Kids. Please visit http://www.battelleforkids.org/networks/p21 for more information.

Note from publisher: Websites change regularly, and their future contents are outside of our control. Supervise children when conducting any recommended online searches for extended learning opportunities.

Printed in the United States of America
Corporate Graphics

TABLE OF CONTENTS

Introduction

What makes sports fun? Fans love watching sports. They love watching great athletes. They love seeing the best in action. They're awed by their skills. They're awed by their talent.

But what makes sports interesting? One never knows what will happen. Fans can expect an outcome. Their side could win. Or their side could lose. Nobody knows for sure.

Sometimes an upset happens. This is when a team that's expected to win loses. Upsets make fans sad. They confuse people.

Sometimes an underdog rises to the top. Underdogs can be players. They can be teams. They have little chance of winning. Yet, they win.

Roberta Vinci runs to the net during a match in 2015, just months before her U.S. Open match against Serena Williams.

Surprises happen. They're shocking. But they're wonderful. They're fun to watch.

That's why games are played. That's why fans watch games. They don't know who's going to win. They don't know who's going to lose. This is the point of sports. Not knowing is exciting.

Upsets in sports are legends. Legends are great stories. They're remembered forever. Underdogs make people smile. They inspire. They give hope. There are many sports champions. The most loved are underdogs. This series is about them.

A joyful Roberta Vinci at the 2015 U.S. Open trophy presentation.

Warming Up

Tennis fans have debated for years. They argue over who's the greatest talent. There's no clear answer. But many agree on Serena Williams. Williams is the best female player. She started in the mid 1990s. She took the sport by storm. She has an older sister. Her sister is Venus. They won many titles. Serena passed Venus as the world's best.

She couldn't be stopped. She crushed tennis. She was on top for many years. At 40, she was still going strong. She showed off her greatness in Grand Slams. These are the 4 biggest tennis games. They're played every year. The first is the Australian Open. It takes place in January. The French Open is in May. Wimbledon is in July. It's in England. The last is the U.S. Open. It's in September.

Venus and Serena Williams at the starts of their careers. Serena went on to become one of the greatest tennis players of all time.

Williams won 23 Grand Slam crowns. She did this before 2022. She almost tied the all-time record. She fell one short. She retired soon after.

Roberta Vinci didn't set any records. She never won a Grand Slam. She was ordinary. She was from Italy. She had played Williams 4 times. This was before the 2015 U.S. Open. She lost each time. She never even won a set. A set is when a player wins 6 games. Women players play best-of-3 sets. The first to win 2 sets wins the match.

Vinci and Williams were ready to meet. They were preparing for the U.S. Open. Williams had already won 3 Grand Slams. She wanted to make history. Only 2 other women had won all 4 in one year.

To win a game, a player must get at least 4 points. And she must win by at least 2 points. Serena Williams and Roberta Vinci had played 8 sets. They did this before the 2015 U.S. Open. None were close. They first met at Wimbledon. This was in 2009. It was the closest match. Williams won the first set 6–4. She won the second 6–3. That was the last Grand Slam they played. But they did compete 3 other times. Williams won a 2012 match. It was in Miami. She won easily. Her scores were 6–2 and 6–1. She beat Vinci again. It was in Paris. It was in 2013. Her scores were 6–1 and 6–3. The two played a month before the 2015 U.S. Open. Nobody thought Vinci could beat Williams. Williams won that match 6–4, 6–3.

The date was September 11, 2015. Vinci had played well. She was in the semifinals. Semifinals are the games that decide who goes to the finals. Vinci and Williams were playing singles tennis semifinals. This means only 4 players are left. Vinci was among the last 4 players. She'd be playing against Williams.

Williams was favored to win. Nobody expected much from Vinci. That is, nobody but Vinci.

Everyone expected Serena Williams to win in her match against Roberta Vinci at the 2015 U.S. Open. Serena had beaten Vinci 4 times in the past.

The Upset

The 2015 U.S. Open had begun. Serena Williams had earned the number 1 seed. A seed is the ranking of players in an event. That came as no surprise. She had won every Grand Slam that year. The Open had 32 seeds. Vinci was not among them. That, too, was not shocking. She wasn't deemed good enough. She played Grand Slams. But she rarely won more than 2 matches.

Roberta Vinci had done better at the U.S. Open. Vinci played well in 2012. She also played well in 2013. But she struggled in 2015. She lost in the first round.

Williams had a strong start in the U.S. Open. She only lost 2 games in her first match. Then she struggled a bit. But she won her next 2 matches. It wasn't easy. She lost a set in the third round. She needed to play her best. She won her next game. She had peaked in time. She was ready to play Vinci.

Roberta Vinci playing at the 2013 U.S. Open. She lost in the quarterfinals to Flavia Pennetta.

That Vinci made it that far was surprising. She lost her second match. She lost badly. She needed 3 sets to win the next round. Then Vinci got lucky. She didn't even have to swing her racket. There was an injury. Her next opponent backed out. Vinci was set to play Williams.

Williams was a much better player. She was given 300–1 odds. Odds are chances something will happen. Williams had a 300 times better chance to win.

Williams was a power player. She hit the ball hard. She smashed it from the baseline. A baseline is the back line on the tennis court. Williams smashed her serve. A serve is an overhead shot. It starts a point or game. Williams smashed her volleys. Volleys are balls that hit the court. They hit near the net. They hit before bouncing.

Williams's power would surely destroy Vinci. No one imagined what happened next.

Billie Jean King was a tennis player. She was incredible. Some believe she was the world's best. She played in the 1960s and 1970s. She won 12 Grand Slam singles titles. She won many others. But King was more than a great player. She fought for women tennis players. She thought they should be paid as much as men. She battled for equal pay. Her most famous match was not against another woman. It was against a man. His name was Bobby Riggs. Riggs said men were better players. King played him in a big event. It was in Houston. It was aired on TV. About 90 million people watched. It was called "The Battle of the Sexes." King won easily. A loss would have been terrible for women's tennis. But she had saved the day. She helped prove that women could do anything.

The Shocker

Serena Williams had a lot on the line. She wanted to win every Grand Slam event in one year. That hadn't been done since 1988. First, she needed to beat Roberta Vinci. A victory would place her in the finals. It was expected to be an easy task. Williams had beaten better players.

Vinci understood that. She knew she couldn't play as usual. She had to perform her best. And even that might not be good enough. She said, "I know that I have a lot of experience. But when you play Serena, it doesn't matter. You have to play better then better then better."

Williams had a wicked serve. It was hard to return.

Vinci had great pressure on her. She had never reached a Grand Slam semifinal. Arthur Ashe Stadium was packed.

Serena Williams wins the 2015 women's singles title at the Australian Open. After this, she won the same title at the French Open and Wimbledon. Her goal was to win every Grand Slam event that year.

The match began. Williams easily won the first set. Vinci only won 2 of 6 games. The battle wasn't over. But nearly everyone felt it was over. One person didn't give up. That was Vinci. She fought back. She gave it everything she had. She sliced shots. Her balls barely bounced. Vinci sent shots barely over the net. Williams couldn't reach them.

Vinci won the second set. Her score was 6–4. It was her first set win ever against Williams. But she still had work to do. She had to win the third set. This would result in an upset. And that is what she did. Vinci needed one more point. She and Williams smashed shots. They did this back and forth. Vinci then dinked one. Her shot barely went over the net. Williams couldn't get to it in time. It was over. She had finally lost. Vinci raised her arms into the air. She shocked everyone. Fans cheered. She had done the impossible. She beat Williams.

Vinci kept playing. She had an average career. But she had beaten Williams. She did this in a Grand Slam semifinal. It was a memory of a lifetime. Nobody could take that away from her.

SAME SPORT, DIFFERENT STORY

Not many players could beat Rafael Nadal. Nadal is a tennis player. He's from Spain. He's among the best ever. He was especially great on clay courts. Balls bounce slower on clay. Nadal waited back for shots. Then, he'd blast them. The French Open is played on clay. Nadal crushed that event. He won it almost every year. He did this from 2005 to 2014. He only lost one game during this time. He lost in 2009. He had played against other superstars. Among them were Roger Federer and Novak Djokovic. Some thought they would've beaten him. But they didn't beat him. It was Robin Söderling. Söderling was from Sweden. Few fans even knew who he was. But they knew in 2009. That was when he stunned Nadal. He easily won the first set. Nadal fought back. He wanted to win the second set. Most expected him to do so. But Söderling had other ideas. He won the third and fourth sets. He beat Nadal. He reached the finals. Then he lost to Federer. But he made tennis history. He had beaten the greatest clay court player ever.

The Response

Roberta Vinci was in a dream world. She had pulled one of the greatest upsets in tennis history. It was a proud moment. She knew many fans wanted Serena Williams to win. She almost felt bad for taking away her Grand Slam. But her pride was much stronger.

She said, "It's an incredible moment for me. It's amazing. It's like a dream. I'm in the final and I beat Serena. I tried to stay focused and not think about the match. Serena's an incredible player. I think it's the best moment of my life."

She had one more game to play. She was to play Flavia Pennetta in the finals. Pennetta is a tennis player. She's from Italy. Vinci and Pennetta have been friends for years. They were friends as children. Neither had ever won a Grand

Roberta Vinci in her match against Serena Williams at the 2015 U.S. Open. Vinci sent shots barely over the net to defeat Serena.

Slam. They were both over 30 years old. Many tennis players retire by that age. And Pennetta was ready to do just that. She told Vinci this would be her last match. Pennetta made it a perfect ending. She beat Vinci. Her scores were 7–6 and 6–2.

Both had earned huge victories at the U.S. Open. Pennetta had taken the title. But some say Vinci had the harder task. She beat Williams. She had achieved the greatest tennis upset ever.

★ Roberta Vinci was born in Taranto. Taranto is in southern Italy. It's on the coast. It's a major port. It has a naval base. Vinci started tennis at age 6. She played for the Taranto Tennis Club.

★ Vinci's father's name is Angelo. He's an accountant. Accountants handle finances. They keep records. They track money. Angelo taught Vinci how to play tennis. He said she had "natural skill."

★ Vinci's mother's name is Luisa. She's a homemaker.

★ Vinci has an older brother. His name is Francesco.

★ Vinci loves coffee. Her favorite is a macchiato. *Macchiato* is an Italian word. It means "marked" or "stained." A macchiato is an espresso with milk. Espresso is dark coffee. Milk stains the coffee. It makes it lighter. It's creamier. That's why it's called a macchiato. When in New York, Vinci gets coffee. She said, "I love to go to this small shop. It has Italian coffee."

Moving On

Perhaps it was the loss to Roberta Vinci. Perhaps it was age catching up to her. Perhaps her opponents were getting better. Maybe it was a bit of all three. But Serena Williams was never the same. She remained a great player. She won Wimbledon in 2016. Her last Grand Slam title was the 2017 Australian Open. She wanted at least 1 more. She had taken 23 Grand Slam events. The all-time record was 24. Williams reached 4 more finals. She did this in 2018 and 2019. She lost them all. She finally retired in 2022. But nothing hurt her legacy. Legacy means how someone is remembered. Many fans believe she was the greatest player ever.

That could not be said about Vinci. She retired in 2018. But she had a good career. Her ranking soared after beating Williams. She reached No. 7 in the world. She finished with 10 titles. They were not Grand Slams. But they were still

Roberta Vinci celebrates her win against Serena Williams. Following this match, she ranked number 7 in the world, and finished her career with 10 titles.

great achievements. She won more matches than she lost. Tennis players earn big money. Vinci won more than $11 million. It was a great career.

She took on a new sport. It's called Padel tennis. It's played on a smaller court. The court is enclosed. Enclosed means surrounded by walls. She became a great professional Padel tennis player. But few people know anything about that game. They know much more about tennis. And they will never forget what Vinci did. They will always remember how she shocked the world.

★ Roberta Vinci toward the beginning of her career, in 2006. She had a great tennis career. She now plays as a professional Padel tennis player.

Learn More

Books

Buckley Jr., James. *Who Are Venus and Serena Williams?* New York, NY: Penguin Workshop, 2017.

Christopher, Matt. *Serena Williams: Legends in Sports*. New York, NY: Little, Brown Books, 2017.

Doeden, Matt. *Coming Up Clutch: The Greatest Upsets, Comebacks, and Finishes in Sports History*. Minneapolis, MN: Millbrook Press, 2018.

Explore These Online Sources with an Adult:

Britannica for Kids: Tennis

Kiddle: Serena Williams Facts for Kids

USTA: Tennis Programs for Kids

Glossary

baseline (BAYS-lyen) Back line of a tennis court

enclosed (en-CLOHZD) Surrounded by walls or closed off on all sides

Grand Slam (GRAND SLAM) One of the 4 most important tennis events played every year

legacy (LEH-guh-see) How a person is remembered

legend (LEH-juhnd) An extremely famous story that is told many times

odds (ODZ) The chances of something happening

seed (SEED) The rankings of players or team for a sporting event

serve (SERV) An overhead shot in tennis

semifinals (SEH-mee-fie-nuhlz) The round of 4 players or teams left in a sporting event

set (SET) Part of a tennis match that requires 6 games won to win

underdog (UNH-der-dawg) A player or team that has little chance of winning but ends up winning

upset (UHP-set) When the team that is expected to win loses

volley (VAHL-ee) A ball in tennis hit before it bounces

Index

About the Author

Martin Gitlin is a sports book author based in Cleveland. He won more than 45 awards as a newspaper sportswriter from 1991 to 2002. Marty has had more than 200 books published since 2006. Most were written for students.